NEW COMPANION TO LENT

All booklets are published thanks to the generous support of the members of the Catholic Truth Society

CATHOLIC TRUTH SOCIETY
PUBLISHERS TO THE HOLY SEE

CONTENTS

Conversion

Conversion is never a once and for all experience: conversion is something fresh every morning, renewed every evening. Our whole Christian life is a process of turning towards God, meeting Him as He comes towards us. No day should pass without refreshing our desire to break with sin, to break away from the values of this world, and to unite ourselves ever more closely to God.

Lent is an opportunity to focus more closely on this work of conversion. Each Lent should bring us one step closer to the Lord, the prayers and works of this year's Lent building on those of last year. Easter should not be the occasion to let slip and abandon all we have built up over those long days of Lent: Easter should be our festival of gratitude for the grace we have experienced and the progress that grace has made in our lives. But we are inconsistent creatures: all our cherished resolutions, our good habits of prayer, our carefully cultivated training and generosity can so easily slip away, dwindle and grow cold. With the best intentions in this world, we cannot keep up a constant fervour of love for God and neighbour: we dwindle, and we need to be refreshed over and over again. That is why the Church gives us the annual cycle of feast and fast, returning regularly to a time of renewal, a time of thanksgiving, a time of steady perseverance which inevitably cools until we need to be renewed again.

Purpose of Lent

What is the real purpose of Lent? Simply this: to help us to love the Lord our God with all our heart, with all soul, with all our strength - and to love our neighbour as ourselves. Nothing else is worthwhile: we are born in order to learn how to love. But love is not easy, and love grows only when we have difficult subjects to work on, when God pretends to be cold and distant so that we have to struggle to keep loving Him, when our neighbours are cold and distant without pretence, and loving them becomes hard work indeed. The progress of our love for God and neighbour is a continual alternation of difficult patches, and gratifying reward, like climbing a flight of stairs. But it is the steep parts that actually get us moving upwards. Lent is a ritualized "riser" of our journey upwards, the difficult struggle to grow in love; Easter is the "tread", the flat part where we can rest, ever careful not to slip back down again.

Historical roots

Historically, Lent seems to have begun as part of the process of welcoming sinners into the Church, a time of preparation before they could be embraced by the sacraments of Easter. Those involved in welcoming them shared in that preparation, and since the entire Christian community should be involved, the entire community came to share in the pattern of prayer, fasting and almsgiving adopted in the period leading up to Easter. When the Church was fresh and new, growing fast, many of these sinners were the new members, the *catechumens* who had made their decision to break with the old way of life and enter the Church. But among them were the old members who had fallen away, and were eager to renew their first fervour, returning from sin towards grace. That is why the public celebration of the sacraments took place during the great ceremonies of Easter: returning sinners were welcomed back on Maundy Thursday, in the sacrament of Penance; new converts embraced on Holy Saturday in Baptism and Confirmation; all united in receiving Holy Communion on Easter Day.

Over the centuries practices changed and developed. During the thousand years when whole nations were solidly Christian and united in the faith, it was rare to welcome new members, since everyone in the community was a Christian from birth. But possibly because of that, not everyone was a good Christian: the sacrament of penance became a necessary part of regular Church life. Although technically that sacrament is only necessary for mortal sin, from the very beginning it had been found extremely useful to practice "confessions of devotion", the regular examination of conscience and discussion of sin before a priest. During the late First Millennium confession and the sacrament of Penance were combined, so that regular confession even of minor faults and tendencies is accompanied by the Church's absolution, not to reconcile one who has fallen far away, but to encourage and strengthen one who wants to keep growing in the love of God and neighbour. There came a time when everyone in the community was encouraged to make their confession and receive absolution every year, at the very beginning of the period of Lent. After this confession all did their penance together, in fasting and prayer, so that the period of Lent was a collective act of thanksgiving for absolution and strengthening for Christian life in the future. From this period dates the name "Shrove Tuesday", for "shrive" was the Middle English word for "absolve", and after the priest "shrived" you, you were "shrove" or "shriven".

Penance

As the Church developed, it became clear that for those who love God more frequent confession was extremely useful. Other seasons (Advent, Embertides) were set aside for confession, followed by a briefer period of fasting and prayer. During the ages when everyone was at least trying to live a Christian life, confession only four times a year was sufficient for many: after all, it was a cleaner age when most people only bathed once a year or so. It was during the turmoil of the Wars of Religion in the sixteenth century, when the unity of the Church was ripped apart, that reforming preachers like St Philip Neri began to encourage much more frequent confession, extending to all Catholics the practices of the early monks. The connection between Lent and confession thus became less obvious, since people go to confession at all times of the year. Nevertheless it is valuable occasionally to make a more lengthy or "general" confession, perhaps looking back over the years to reflect on what grace has achieved, as well as assessing what still needs to be done. The beginning of Lent would be an appropriate time for that. (I stress the beginning not just for historical reasons, but because confessionals become very busy at the end of Lent, as those who still only bathe once a year crowd in for their "Easter duties". The very concept of "Easter duties", a burdensome obligation to confess and communicate only once a year, indicates a love of God with rather less than whole heart and soul and strength, a bare minimum just sufficient to keep you inside the Church!)

Fasting

For many centuries, the practice of fasting during Lent was taken very seriously in the Western Church, as it still is in the Eastern. It was only really during the terrible wars of the twentieth century that fasting was slackened off: when all food was rationed there was no possibility of fasting; when meat was unobtainable you ate whale and were grateful for it. The return of peace, such as it was, never brought about a return to pre-war Lenten fasting. As a result what the Church actually requires of us is very little indeed, so that when Eastern Christians or Muslims ask us whether we practice fasting, we are embarrassed to answer. But it was not always so. For centuries, all Catholics abstained from eating meat on all weekdays of Lent, and at certain periods abstained from dairy products as well. That is why the last remaining butter and eggs were used up for pancakes on Shrove Tuesday, and it was known in French speaking countries as "Fat Tuesday", *Mardi Gras*. The Italians were more conscious of saying farewell to meat: *carne*, *vale*.

Ash Wednesday

Now we begin Lent with Ash Wednesday. It is not a holy day of obligation, but more people come to Mass that day than on any other weekday. During the Mass the readings speak of repentance, of making a new start; "come back to me with all your heart", says the Lord. We mark that repentance with the sign of ashes, blessed and imposed on the forehead as a sign that we have turned away from sin to believe in the Gospel, that we are dust and unto dust we shall return. It emphasizes our weakness and nothingness, as well as the fact that we embrace the Good News that we have been redeemed and saved, we are now children of God and heirs to the Kingdom.

The forty days

Lent is always defined as "forty days": now if you start counting on Ash Wednesday you will reach the fortieth day on Holy Saturday if you omit the Sundays. Sundays do not count as Lent: they remain the celebration of the Lord's Resurrection, even though in the Western Church we still keep the Lenten colour and austerity in the liturgy. Actually the Annunciation, 25th March, nearly always comes in Lent and is a solemnity when Lent is suspended; the Italians may also take St Joseph's day off, and the Irish St Patrick's. Lent ends with the first Alleluia of the Easter Vigil. Before 1952 that was sung on Holy Saturday morning: now it must be after dark on the following evening. It isn't really the number forty that matters, it is the idea of a season of renewal of our commitment to the love of God and neighbour, our decisive rejection of the values of this world.

The Gospels make it abundantly clear that the way to salvation is quite contrary to the ways of this world. Not that God hates the world, far from it: "God so loved the world that he gave his only Son... that the world might be saved through him" (*Jn* 3:16-17). But this world has rejected God, has turned away from truth and beauty and unity, and does everything it can to attack and destroy the faith of God's people. There is a great deal about that in Our Lord's discourses at the Last Supper (*Jn* 4-17). We cannot be under any illusions: either we serve this world and its passing fashions, or we serve God and model our lives on Jesus Christ. Being a Christian has always meant standing apart from the world we live in, never more so than in our own time. Christians have different values, different priorities. Lent is an opportunity to refresh our determination to follow God's way, and to reject the paths of this world. No one ever said it would be easy: "the gate is wide and the way is easy that leads to destruction, and those who enter by it are many. For the gate is narrow and the way is hard, that leads to life, and those who find it are few" (*Mt* 7:13-14).

Fasting

The first element of our Lenten exercise is *fasting*. In the broad sense, fasting means any act of self-denial, a conscious decision not to give in to the whim of the moment, or be driven by appetites, passions and hormones, but to take control of our own lives. In other words, fasting is a radical declaration of freedom. But we do so, not to build up our own ego, and strengthen our own characters for our own self-aggrandizement - that would just be giving in to a different sort of passion. No, we fast in order to forget ourselves and concentrate on God and our neighbour. Fasting must be directed outwards, away from self. Otherwise it is just slimming. Of course a result of fasting will be health and beauty, with a strong and attractive character, but if that is our conscious motive we will fail disastrously in the attempt. The motive, as for everything else we do, must be the love of God and the love of neighbour.

In St Luke's Gospel, Our Lord speaks very severely indeed about the appropriate punishment for child-molesters, and then immediately afterwards about the need to be constantly forgiving (*Lk* 17:1-4). He is not contradicting Himself: He is teaching us that forgiveness does not mean the remission of punishment. Sin deserves punishment: if we refuse to repent, and we deliberately reject the love of God, then we have the terrible freedom to exclude ourselves from God's love for all eternity. It is our choice. If we do repent and come back seventy seven times a day, God forgives us at once, but there still needs to be some correction. That is what the Church calls the "temporal punishment due to sin", the debt we must pay, either through penance in this life, or after this life in Purgatory. Of course we may, and are strongly encouraged to, carry each others' burdens, by taking on ourselves the penance due to others. Moreover we are encouraged to apply to the Church for a share in the all-sufficient merits of Christ, joined with the merits of all the saints, that we call the "treasury of the Church", dispersed in the form of Indulgences. (See the *Catechism of the Catholic Church*, 1459-60, 1471-3).

Fasting as Penance

Fasting is a manner of doing penance. Now the Church has never encouraged extravagant and competitive penances, doing severe things to ourselves in the hope of impressing God and our neighbours. Our Lord tells us to keep our fasting secret and not to draw attention to ourselves (*Mt* 6:16-18). St Paul develops the metaphor of training for a sporting event: we discipline our bodies for the sake of being able to achieve what we desire, not a mere sporting trophy but the crown of eternal life (1 *Cor*

9:24-7). There have been phases in the history of the Church when certain penitential practices became popular, and people competed with each other as to how vigorously they could carry them out. St Jerome tells of disedifying competitions among hermits in the desert to see how long they could go without eating anything at all. In the twelfth century they took to wearing shirts of horse-hair that tickled and itched and provided a home for all sorts of small creatures. In the fifteenth century there was a craze for self-flagellation, and gangs of penitents would wander through the streets whipping themselves. The saints have always been wary of such excesses, and taught their followers a less ostentatious and more salutary approach to penance. St John Cassian stresses that fasting must not damage the health, otherwise one becomes useless in the service of God or neighbour. St Philip Neri strongly discouraged things like hair shirts (by insisting that they should be worn over the other garments), and restricted the use of the "discipline" to very short periods in total privacy.

The best penances have always been the ones God chooses for us. Cheerful and willing acceptance of the innumerable difficulties, inconveniences and aggravations of everyday life, is worth very much more than a complicated exercise of our own devising. It is not penitential to grumble endlessly about the circumstances of our life, while practising some bizarre form of self-restraint. True self-restraint lies in the turning of necessity into virtue, as St Francis de Sales used to say. Other people will provide us with plenty of opportunities for mortifying our desires and restraining our appetites.

Nevertheless, it is still essential in the Christian life to practice some form of deliberate voluntary self-mortification. The most obvious and the most traditional area is in matters of food and drink.

Food and drink

The Church actually *requires* remarkably little of us. Two days a year, Ash Wednesday and Good Friday, are days of technical *fasting*. That means that we have only one major cooked meal in the day, with two light snacks. In addition we *abstain*, which means not eating meat on those days. In the modern world, a great many people never eat more than that anyway, and abstain from meat altogether. The general rule of the Church is also to abstain from meat every Friday (except a major solemnity), although this may be varied in different countries, and in Britain alternative exercises can be substituted. Again, this is no more than many people do anyway. Before receiving Holy Communion the Church also requires one hour's fast (except for the sick). At a Sunday Mass of normal length that means merely not eating during Mass. The requirements seem to be so trivial that we instinctively feel we ought to do more. But that immediately leads us into the danger of ostentation, of pride in being better and stricter than everyone else. We do have to be careful in how we fast, so as not to come under Our Lord's condemnation of the hypocrites.

So what can we do? There are three possible ways in which we can mortify our appetites for food and drink, each of which can be practised without drawing attention to ourselves. Ideally the person sitting next to you at table should not be able to detect what your Lenten fast is.

Eat less

The first is simply eating less. If we take one spoonful of potatoes rather than three, a smaller portion of pudding than we immediately feel we want, only one biscuit with our morning coffee, we have to remind ourselves at every course of every meal that we are trying to keep Lent, and at every course we will be allowing ourselves just a little bit less than we first thought we would like. If we can keep that up for the whole of Lent, it will become easier, almost second nature: which means that the next Lent we can be just that little bit more abstemious. But we must remember the warning of Cassian and the other saints that if we reduce our consumption of food to the extent that our health suffers, then we are going to become a burden on our neighbours who will have to look after us, and we will find it more and more difficult to pray: the end result will be quite the opposite of what we wanted, which was love of God and neighbour. Different people have different capacities and needs: in a hot climate one needs to eat far less than in a cold region where most of the food is needed just to keep up the body temperature. That is why laying down rules about quantities and weights is not really helpful.

Basic fare

Here is where the second form of fasting comes in: it consists of choosing simpler and cheaper foods. In the modern world we are faced with such a huge choice of foods, products that used to be rare and exotic beckoning us from the shelves of the supermarket. We are always being tempted by something new, something choice and luxurious. A deliberate decision to go for ordinary foods, and basic fare, means again that every day we have the opportunity to mortify the appetites. Choosing mushy peas instead of guacamole, pickled onions instead of quails' eggs, brings us down to earth and reminds us of the value of simple things. I hesitate to speak of sharing the diet of the poor, because in Britain now the most exotic things are brought within the reach of the poorest, and indeed many of the most disadvantaged people are short of money precisely because they do spend too much on fancy foods. A diet of pre-prepared meals and "junk food" is not cheap, but eating more cheaply may involve a little more time spent peeling spuds or soaking beans!

But in a world where everyone is aware of everyone else, it is worth reminding ourselves of poverty in other countries, where a simple bowl of porridge is as much as anyone can hope for.

No snacks

The third form of fasting recommended by the early saints is very simply not eating between meals. If you have a fixed timetable of mealtimes, breakfast, dinner and supper, or whatever pattern you choose, then stick to it. Eat nothing before the set time, nothing after it. That can be very difficult in the modern world, where fixed mealtimes have all but disappeared from peoples' lives, and many seem to spend the entire day grazing from one snack to another. It means, therefore, disciplining ourselves in terms of time as well as food, again making a conscious decision to live in a way different from that of so many people around us. It was also suggested recently that it would be a good idea to return voluntarily to the older practice of not eating solid food for three hours before Holy Communion, as a way of making ourselves aware of what we are preparing to do. Now everything I have said about food applies equally to drink. Curiously the Church has never suggested abstaining from alcohol as a penitential exercise, but it seems an obvious thing to recommend these days, when so many people suffer from the effects of drink. We can decide to drink less, rationing ourselves strictly to a certain amount; or we can decide to drink something cheap and simple - something in a screw-top bottle instead of a rare vintage - or we can be strict about never drinking outside set hours, never before the sun is over the yardarm. In practice many people find it a valuable discipline to give up alcoholic drinks altogether during Lent. That has now become much easier, even among friends - you only have to dangle a set of car keys at a party for people to be sympathetic, and they won't pressurize you to drink the way they would have thirty years ago.

All these forms of fasting have the unintentioned side effect that you will be generally rather fitter, happier and nicer to live with than you would have been if you just gave in to every appetite for food and drink whenever you felt like it. But that, as I said, must not be the motive for fasting, it is just the Lord's way of showing His love for us. You will also save a great deal of money: I shall come to suggestions on what to do with that money later.

Approach to entertainment

Fasting from food and drink may be the most obvious and traditional Lenten exercise, but the modern world provides us with plenty of other opportunities for self-discipline that may be equally valuable or more so. So often we find ourselves wasting time simply looking for entertainment, flicking over television programmes that we find boring and distasteful, viewing DVDs of poor-quality films, aimlessly surfing the Internet in the search for amusement, while trying to persuade ourselves that it is educational. What would happen if we decided to apply the three types of fasting to our search for entertainment? We could strictly ration the amount of time spent viewing or surfing, reducing the time from the national average of three hours a day to an hour and a half. Or we could be determined to choose only wholesome programmes or websites, selecting with care only what might be genuinely educational. Or we could be adamant in never watching or surfing before a set time of the evening, and finishing smartly at the time we have chosen. Maybe on Fridays in Lent the screen could be switched off altogether. There are endless possibilities for the development of self-control in these areas, for the individual or for the family. And again, there are side-effects: better physical health, better posture if we are not endlessly hunched over the keyboard, less distracting thoughts and memories to lead our minds into unwholesome channels. Whatever we choose to do in the way of self-denial seems to have the result that we actually improve in character and happiness. As St John of the Cross put it, if you want to be everything, seek to be nothing! And of course self-discipline in watching and viewing and surfing will give us a lot of spare time. I shall come to suggestions on what to do with that time later.

Be inspired

It is not difficult in the life of each one of us to think of useful alternative forms of fasting. Some may decide to give up buying books during Lent; others may resolve to read only non-fiction, or only novels by Catholic authors. Some will find it best to cut down on gambling, refraining from playing the lottery during the weeks of Lent, or betting only on horses with Catholic owners... We can use our imagination as well as our sense of humour in choosing what we are going to do for Lent, bearing in mind always the essential points: we do not do it to attract attention, we do not do it for the sake of the health, time or money we shall gain, we do it because we want to love God and our neighbour, and we really want to turn away from sin and believe the Good News.

ALMSGIVING

The second essential element in our Lenten exercise is *almsgiving*, which means any sort of practical charity towards other people. Without charity, all our faith, prayer and fasting, spirituality and learning, self-control and ostentatious virtue goes for nothing. Charity is the tangible proof that we do have faith (see *Jas* 2:14-26, and 1 *Cor* 13). We might be able to convince ourselves that we love God, but we cannot persuade ourselves or anyone else that we love our neighbour if we really do not. Christianity is tested by its practical results - "see how these Christians love one another!"

Charity in thought and word

Now charity must be practised in thought, word, deed and omission. We can begin very easily by making ourselves think charitable thoughts, reflecting on the good qualities of those irritating people around us. When we find our thoughts coming back again and again to people who have hurt us, people whose way of life offends us, people who annoy us by being more successful than us... why, then is the time to make ourselves think of some little point in their favour. And then it becomes that much easier to say the right thing, to utter some words of encouragement or congratulation, to tell the good news about other people's good qualities. We can spread a lot of happiness that way. That too is where charity by omission comes in: often charity requires silence, omitting to say the clever remark or the stinging comment. To be honest, some people are best loved at a distance: when we see them or remember them we should say a quick silent Hail Mary for them and then deliberately think of something quite different.

Nevertheless, because the purpose of our life is learning to love, God will always make sure there is someone close to us who is difficult to love, so we can practice. It is usually someone in the family, the workplace, the community. Charity, in reality, *ends* at home. It is much easier to love enemies whom we never meet, and strangers who live far away, than it is to love those whom we have to face across the breakfast table every morning. If we begin by trying to think charitable thoughts about Osama bin Laden or Robert Mugabe, we can work up gradually to charity towards the mother-in-law.

Practical almsgiving

However charity in thought and word is not the same as almsgiving: that means something practical. It means being generous with our time, our money and ourselves, to give effective help to those who need it, whether they are near us or far away. That in turn means a radical break with the standards of the world around us. We live in a world devoted entirely to the process of making money, which judges everything in commercial terms. It is a world that is quite ruthless towards those who through their own stupidity, or as a result of our own shrewd business dealings, have found themselves at a disadvantage. It is a world that rejoices in philosophies and superstitions that reassure us that the poor deserve to be poor and that God favours the rich. That is the world we must repudiate if we are to be Christians. Our Lord was radical indeed when He said "Blessed are the poor", and "it will be hard for a rich man to enter the Kingdom of Heaven" (*Lk* 6:20; *Mt* 19:23). The apostles were astounded, because they had been brought up on the idea that God favours the wealthy and powerful, and ever since then many have tried to shy away from the plain sense of the Gospel, but there is no getting round it. "The love of money", says St Paul, "is the root of all evils" (1 *Tim* 6:10). While not all Christians are called to a life of total poverty like St Francis, all are obliged to treat material goods only as means to an end, which is, as always, the love of God and neighbour. There have been rich saints, like St Joseph of Arimathea, who used their wealth generously and prudently to benefit others, but the rich man who gathers wealth only for himself finds no comfort in the Gospels (*Lk* 16:19-31).

Ways of giving

Practical almsgiving can take many forms. The poor are with us always, and the needs of other people are constantly brought to our attention. Charity need not involve actual money: much can be done simply by giving time and skill. Those unable to leave home can keep busy and be useful just by knitting old wool from unravelled jerseys into blankets for the Missionaries of Charity. There is a lot that can be done even if we are unable to walk or to leave home. Many voluntary organisations need people who can address envelopes or recycle Christmas cards or do simple secretarial work from the comfort of their own laptop. No one can really claim to be too poor, too old or too disabled to perform any act of kindness. In reality, as every voluntary organisation knows, it is precisely the poor and disadvantaged who are always the most generous. Persuading the rich and busy that they ought to help is much more difficult!

Moving on to more energetic forms of practical charity, in every part of our country there are people in need, and there are opportunities for helping them. The gap between rich and poor has become wider and wider over the last generation, and more and more people slip through the net of the comprehensive system of public benefits that was constructed in the 1940s. They may now depend entirely on the almsgiving of the charitable.

Charity to beggars

The first and most immediate challenge to our charity is in the young beggars that can be found in almost every town and city of Britain. But here at once we need to remember the cardinal virtue of prudence. Nearly all the street beggars that we encounter are severely dependent on drugs or alcohol. That does not mean we should not be sympathetic and helpful: it may be "their own fault" but which of us has not at some time got into difficulties through our own fault, and were grateful to friends who helped us out of them? And which of us does not have some family member who at some time has had difficulties with alcohol or drugs? Nevertheless a gift of money will usually only keep the beggar in that state of dependency, and will do nothing to help him out of it. Worse than that, the profits from drug dealings ultimately go to finance international terrorism, so that by giving directly to a street beggar you may be collaborating in the death and destruction of the innocent. Most people who work with the street homeless agree that the only effective way to help is to give your money to the organisations and agencies that provide a welcome, a shelter, food, washing and clothing, access to medical care, and the long process of rehabilitation that really does enable them to shake off the dependency and become again the sort of people they would really like to be. In any town it is not difficult to find the address of the relevant agencies; in some places there is a general umbrella fund that will distribute contributions to the different agencies for you. The immediate response to the street beggar in person then has to be a kind word and a smile, and the offer to take them to the nearest drop-in centre or shelter - though they will not thank you for this as they will already be perfectly well aware of them! That is one of the first tests of true charity: we go on trying to help even when the people we are helping don't want us!

The agencies and organisations I have mentioned also need practical help. Unfortunately at present any sort of voluntary work is so restricted by new regulations and red-tape that most people will be unable to do anything that involves actually meeting the poor or disadvantaged, but there is still scope for quiet work behind the scenes, fund-raising, secretarial help, the design and placing of posters. If we have saved some time by fasting from television, or saved some money by eating more cheaply, then there are plenty of opportunities for using that time and money to good effect locally.

Discernment in giving aid to organizations

But of course the needs of people in our own country are insignificant compared to the poverty of many people overseas. We may wonder what one person can do to help, but one and one and one add up, and in the absence of effective governmental help, the large-scale voluntary organisations do actually make a lot of difference. For most of us the only way we can give alms overseas is by giving money to one of these organisations. It is worth being selective, and prudent: not every aid-organisation can be trusted to use the money well. Some are committed to the cynical idea that the only thing necessary is to prevent poor people from breeding, thus ensuring that the rich can continue to monopolise the world's resources. Any project that ties aid to compulsory sterilisation, abortion or contraception is demeaning to the human rights of the people they are allegedly trying to help, telling them in effect that they have no right to exist and should be gently exterminated. In the struggle against AIDS the policy of scattering condoms over Africa like landmines has proved totally ineffective, as infection rates continue to rise - the only areas where there has been any success in controlling the infection is where they have applied Catholic or Islamic teaching about abstinence and fidelity. So choose your aid organisation carefully, and support it well. Something specifically Catholic like "Aid to the Church in Need" can be relied on to direct funds properly.

And even in the case of distant poverty giving money is not the only option: we can do effective fund-raising or administrative work without leaving home. A few of us may have the opportunity to travel and actually help people where they live, but again that needs to be done with prudence in order to be really effective. Simply buying a ticket to an earthquake zone and breezing in, all smiles and goodwill, may not actually be very helpful where food is already in short supply. Voluntary work overseas does need to be properly planned, and the well-established agencies do know what they are doing!

Without love, nothing

Whether our almsgiving is at home or overseas, we do need to remember what Our Lord said about the hypocrites (*Mt* 6:2-4). Ideally the person we are helping should not know who is giving the money, which is why putting it anonymously into a collection box has its merits. On the other hand if there would be a significant tax advantage by giving it through CAF or Gift-Aid, then it would be silly not to use the opportunity, but it can still be kept secret between you and the tax collectors. The motive is not our own self-esteem, still less the admiration of others; the motive can be nothing but love, the love of God whom we cannot see made flesh in the love of the neighbour whom we might be able to see. Charity, almsgiving, covers a multitude of sins (1 *Pet* 4:8) and is an important weapon in our struggle against selfishness. Fasting without almsgiving may be very selfish indeed: the two together expiate our sins and unite us to the love of God.

Prayer

Without *prayer*, everything else is meaningless. Indeed, without prayer we would have no motivation to keep Lent at all, let alone try to fast or give alms. We might imagine that works of charity can stand on their own without prayer, but unless we have the primary motivation of the Love of God, our love for His more unattractive creatures will very rapidly dwindle away. (That is not to deny that there are good atheists who can be genuinely kind to others, but their goodness is doubtless the work of the Holy Spirit calling them without their knowledge. By and large leading atheists like Enver Hoxha or Mao Tse Tung were not noted for selfless benevolence.) We cannot truly practice the love of God without being forced to love our neighbour: that is why prayer really comes first among our Lenten exercises.

How to pray

Prayer was defined by St John Damascene as "the raising of the heart and mind to God" (quoted in *Catechism*, 2559). It is not so much a question of telling God things, or asking Him for things, but of listening to Him, and allowing Him to mould us into the image of his will. There are many different ways of praying, because we all differ so much, and during a lifetime we will find that different forms of prayer are appropriate at different times. The golden rule is "pray as you can and don't try to pray as you can't" (Abbot Chapman). We should not be bullied into praying in a way that is wrong for us just because other people find it very helpful, nor should we disparage other peoples' methods of prayer and try to impose our own on them. Unless we have agreed to use some specific form of prayer (for example by joining a fraternity or Third Order) we are perfectly free to pray in whatever manner we find most effective. How do we judge effectiveness? Simply over whether it helps us to love God and neighbour.

Vocal prayer

The most obvious form of prayer is *vocal prayer*, using words to express ourselves before God. We may use long-established set forms of words, beginning of course with the Our Father, the Hail Mary, the familiar prayers of childhood, going on to use the Psalms, the prayers composed by the saints, modern books of prayers for all occasions. Or we may choose our own words, engaging in a conversation with God. But the thing to remember is that really all these words are addressed by God to us, not the other way round. Many saints have written commentaries on the Our Father, taking us through it word by word; perhaps the best known are the ones by St Cyprian and St Augustine, used for the Office of Readings (in Weeks 11 and 29) and St Teresa of Avila (from the *Way of Perfection*, often printed as a separate pamphlet). They remind us that every word is intended to change us: it is we who must keep God's name holy, and form His kingdom, and do His will; it is we who must forgive others that we might be forgiven. When we pray we are asking God to conform us to become what we want to be, true heirs of the Kingdom. We certainly must pray for our needs in this world, our daily bread, but we can rely on our heavenly Father to know what they are. We do not need to produce long and eloquent compositions telling God exactly what is wrong with His world and how we can advise Him to put it right - that is the sort of prayer the pagans use, as Our Lord says (*Mt* 6:7). Words can be very useful in prayer, but we must listen to them, not just utter them.

The Psalms

From the very beginning the Church has found the Psalms invaluable in prayer. Every human mood is there, joy and gratitude, hope and entreaty, compassion and encouragement - not forgetting anger and frustration. The modern Divine Office has tamed the Psalms, omitting certain passages which might be thought upsetting for modern readers, but it is worth reading them in full, to understand that true prayer must include our darker moments. Whatever mood we are in, that is how we must appear before God. We cannot deceive Him by pretending to be all sweetness and light if we are really seething with anger; only if we are honest in facing up to our anger, then He can change us. Psalm 108/9 has its place still! For two thousand years the recitation of the Divine Office meant reading or chanting every word of the Psalms every week, bringing all human experience before God.

Distractions in prayer

But how, you will ask, can anyone attend to the meaning and listen to every word of the 150 Psalms? That brings us at once to the problem of *distractions* during prayer. It is a truth universally acknowledged that however good our intentions, we cannot guarantee that our attention will remain steady for as much as a minute at a time. St Bernard tells the story of the beggar who demanded alms of a knight, and the knight said he could have his horse if he could say one Our Father without distraction. But the beggar had only got as far as "Hallowed be Thy name" before breaking off to ask if he got the saddle too. The mind will wander off after all sorts of trivial, inappropriate or even indecent topics. St Teresa admits that her attention wandered off during the Divine Office, and was advised to take no notice of it. "I advise you to do the same, for I believe the evil is incurable" (*Letters*, no. 400, 9 Oct.

1581). When we realize we have been distracted, we should never worry, but take no notice of it. Except that it is humiliating, and humility is a very good thing. And the subjects of our involuntary distraction may form a useful examination of conscience. As a rule, what matters is not the *attention* but the *intention* - as long as we began our prayer with a real desire to pray, God goes on listening even when we don't.

Meditation

Distractions remain a problem, even in other forms of prayer. For many people a fruitful method is to use the Scriptures, or another spiritual writing, as a basis for intellectual thought, pondering over the meaning of what we are reading, thinking out what it is telling us about God, and ourselves, and how we should relate to others. This is classically called *meditation*, using the conscious mind. We may take a Gospel passage (for instance the one set for the daily or Sunday Mass), imagine ourselves as part of the scene, think of the setting, the different characters, the words of Our Lord. We think what He is saying to the disciples, what He is saying to the Church now, what He is saying to me in particular this morning. We resolve to listen to Him, and act on His words. We conclude with gratitude and love. We may find it useful to keep the book open in front of us throughout the time of meditation, or to write points down as they occur to us.

Meditation on a text differs from ordinary reading, in that we may find one or two verses of the Gospel, or one paragraph of our spiritual book, enough for half an hour. Ordinary reading at other times is tremendously valuable to feed the mind with the knowledge of God, though there too we need not try to read books that really do not suit us: there is quite enough variety available among the writings of the saints.

Prayer of the heart

For many people, set words and long prayers are no help at all: they prefer to use short phrases, repeated frequently. These phrases, *aspirations*, may be a verse of Scripture, like "O God come to my assistance, O Lord make haste to help me", or "Jesus, Son of the Living God, have mercy on me, a sinner". We can repeat them over and over again, using the rhythm of the words to quieten down the teeming mind, so that the heart is free to gaze at God. Or we can use them at intervals during the business of the day, continually pinning the day to heaven, reminding ourselves that God is with us at every moment. The Rosary naturally finds its place here. Repeated phrases in prayer is one of the gateways to silent *contemplation*, when the words gradually cease to be necessary, and we can simply remain still in the presence of God, aware only of His love for us. By no means everyone can contemplate, but for those who can, any form of words or method of meditation is a waste of time, and will not help. St Teresa explains that this is because once you have found God, you no longer need to search for Him with the intellect (*Interior Castle*, VII, 9). Very often it is children and uneducated people who can most easily remain still in perfect contemplation of God, without the distractions of too much information cluttering up the mind. We think of the blacksmith who sat for hours looking at the tabernacle, and told St John Vianney "I look at Him, and He looks at me".

It doesn't matter which form of prayer you choose, or what time of day you pray, though every day must contain at least one period of prayer. What matters, indeed what is absolutely essential for the Christian life, is that you do pray. And when we pray, we can be aware that the entire Church prays with us, the angels and the saints joining us in one great chorus of praise and thanksgiving to the God who loves us so much.

How to make a Retreat

Christianity is not a religion that can be lived in isolation. 'Love your neighbour as yourself' is Jesus' greatest commandment, and he tells us that we are to be 'the light of the world and the salt of the earth' (*Mt* 5:13-14). It is in the world, alongside other people, that we are called to live our faith in Jesus Christ.

Why a retreat?

Nevertheless, it is right that from time to time we should step back from the 'ordinary' world, and the pressures of everyday life, and spend a little time focussing exclusively on our relationship with God. Indeed, we read that Jesus himself, although he lived entirely for others, retired from time to time to be alone with his heavenly Father - for example the night before he chose his 12 Apostles (*Lk* 6:12-17), and on the eve of his saving Passion (*Mk* 14:36). Going on retreat is one way in which we can spend some time alone with God, building up our relationship with him and drawing strength to live as good Christians in a frequently hostile world. While on retreat, as Pope Benedict XVI said in one of his early homilies 'people can again find their true dimension - they rediscover themselves as creatures, small but at the same time unique'.

We might also think of an ordinary human relationship. A husband and wife who never spend time together are unlikely to have long years of happily married life - their union will grow weak and falter. Similarly, our faith can weaken and die unless we sometimes give time generously to our relationship with the Lord.

What sort of retreat?

There are many sorts of retreat we can chose from - there is something to suit every personality or spiritual need (further information is given below). Broadly, we can divide retreats into three categories. A 'preached' retreat involves joining a group of people and attending regular talks, or 'spiritual conferences', given by a retreat director, who could be a priest, a religious sister or, indeed, a lay-person. The director would probably not see people individually, but time would be given for those on retreat to reflect on what they have heard and absorb it personally. An individually directed retreat, on the other hand, involves seeing a retreat director for a personal meeting at least once or twice a day. The director will help the retreatant to choose scripture passages, readings and forms of prayer which he hopes will meet their own particular spiritual needs at a given moment. Some of these directed retreats have a special theme, involving art, music etc. Finally, it is also possible for individuals to go somewhere for a period, most often to a monastery or convent, where they can take part in the daily liturgy, and make a private retreat. This is done without a director, and relies on spiritual reading, set times of prayer and involvement in the liturgical life of the community to nourish the individual's intimacy with God.

Making a good retreat

Given the enormous variety in the retreats on offer, it would be impossible to offer 'rules' which would apply in every case. If you do decide to make a retreat, you need to decide what form of retreat would suit you best, and then make a resolution to enter whole-heartedly into this encounter with God, asking him to bless this special time. Here are a few questions which might be asked, and which apply to most forms of retreat.

How long should a retreat be?

As long as you need (or can spare)! Even a single day spent out of our normal routine, with time given to prayer, can be very profitable. However, to give ourselves time to adjust to a different routine, and to allow God to draw us to himself and speak to our hearts, a longer period is preferable. A week would be very suitable.

Where can I go?

Again, there are a vast variety of places to chose from. Ideas are given below. You will obviously chose somewhere which offers a form of retreat which meets your needs and which it is practical for you to get to. It is wise, if possible, to leave our local neighbourhood, in order to help create 'distance' from our ordinary routines - a space that God can then fill. However, avoid going somewhere so distant that you will arrive exhausted and return exhausted from travelling. It is also unwise to choose a location purely because we like the weather, the scenery or because we can fit in some sight-seeing nearby - a retreat can indeed be a recreation for body and soul, but it is not to be confused with a holiday!

Appropriate books and prayers?

Again, much depends on the form of retreat you choose. If you have an individual director, he or she will advise you. If you are part of a 'preached' retreat, you will want to give time to reflecting on the director's conferences - and he or she will probably recommend prayers and readings themselves. Obviously a bible is indispensable!

If you are making a 'private' retreat alone, then you will probably find that the retreat centre or religious house you are staying in will have a collection of spiritual books you can use. St Philip Neri, a great director of souls in the Sixteenth Century, used to say we should always prefer spiritual books by authors whose names began with 'S' - in other words, the Saints! *The Introduction to the Devout Life*, by St Francis de Sales is a great spiritual classic, and can be returned to again and again. St Ignatius Loyola, the founder of the Jesuits, wrote *The Spiritual Exercises*, which would provide the structure for a whole retreat - however, this book is best used with the help of an experienced Ignatian retreat director. Of course, there are many excellent contemporary books as well. *Searching for God*, by the late Cardinal Basil Hume is a good place to begin.

Whatever form of retreat you choose, you will hopefully be able to make daily Mass the centre of your day. Any Catholic site offering retreats should provide daily Mass, and it is at the Eucharist that we will draw close to God in a unique way. If staying in a religious community which sings the Divine Office, do take the opportunity to attend some or all of the Offices. Taking part in the official Prayer of the Church is another source of grace not to be missed. Finally, a retreat is also a good time to celebrate the Sacrament of Reconciliation – to make a good confession. It might also be a good opportunity to make a 'General Confession' – to look back over your whole life and to offer God your repentance for the times you have not stayed close to him.

Do I need to keep silent the whole time?

Silence is an important part of any retreat - indeed, an important part of prayer. Our modern world is full of words and noise - from the buzz of the internet to the taped music in shopping malls. Very often, all these words can drive out God. We do need sometimes to keep silence, and it is precisely in this time of quiet that we will hear God speaking to us.

That said, retreats will differ in the amount of silence required. Some will be almost entirely silent, others more relaxed. Either way, do try and spend at least some periods in total quiet with God. A lot of people find this difficult, but it is part of the generosity of spirit we should bring to this time of retreat. Try to avoid the idle chatter we fill so much of our day with. Similarly, it is best to avoid (for just a few short days!) reading the daily newspapers, watching television, or resorting to mobile phones or laptops. We will not get much out this time of retreat, if we insist on bringing the world along with us!

Ideas and further reading

The Retreat Association (www.retreats.org) and The Good Retreat Guide (by Stafford Whiteaker, pub. Rider and Co.) offer a wide range of possibilities. Not all the sites listed are Catholic, or suitable for Catholics, but it may help give you ideas.

The Jesuits specialise in personally directed retreats in the spirit of their founder, St Ignatius. Find out more at www.jesuit.org

Many Benedictine monasteries and convents welcome lay-people who want to make a retreat. You can find your nearest Benedictine house by consulting the *Benedictine Yearbook*.

Making a Good Confession

The need for forgiveness

All of us, as human beings, are weak, frail, imperfect - we are sinners. And all of us, at some level, long for forgiveness. In Confession, God has given us a wonderful opportunity to receive it. No sin we could commit is too great to be forgiven - for God's love for us is infinite, and his mercy boundless. All he asks of us is to come humbly to this sacrament of mercy and reconciliation and to receive from him the pardon he longs to give.

Why do I need a priest?

Whenever the Sacrament of Reconciliation (Confession) is discussed, this question is bound to arise. 'Why do I need a priest?' 'Why do we need a *Sacrament* of Reconciliation?'. People ask why they cannot simply confess their sins to God in private, rather than telling them to the priest.

The first thing to say is that in our private prayers we should indeed examine our conscience, and if we have committed any sins, great or small, we should say sorry to God for them straight away, with a simple act of contrition. The Church encourages us to examine our conscience daily - indeed, the 'Examination of Conscience' forms the opening of Compline, part of the official Prayer of the Church. If people do regularly keep an account of their sins in this way, then they will find it much easier, and more rewarding, when they come to make a Sacramental Confession.

But simply 'saying sorry' to God in our private prayers is never enough. The Sacrament of Confession is about much more than that. At one level, we should remember that we are all members of the Church. When we sin, therefore, we offend the Church in some way. It is only appropriate that a minister of the Church (the priest) gives us absolution. But, at a deeper level, we also need to reflect that the Sacrament of Confession, like every sacrament, is about *change*. In this case, the change is in us. We don't simply say sorry to God - our sins are forgiven, blotted out, removed, annihilated. We are given the chance of a fresh start, a new beginning, in a way which is quite unique in our human experience. Not only that, but every sacrament is also a channel of God's grace - his love and strength, the lifeblood of our souls. Confession, too, brings us this grace - God's assistance, which not only forgives our sins but helps us to avoid sin in future. Confession should not be seen simply as a 'last resort' when things have gone wrong, but as an essential element in our journey towards heaven.

How often should I go?

The simple answer is - as often as you need to! The Church makes a sensible distinction between 'mortal' sins and 'venial' sins. A mortal sin has three characteristics - it must be something very serious, that we knew was wrong, and that we gave our full consent to doing. If we are aware that we have committed a mortal sin, we should go to Confession as soon as possible (and we should refrain from taking Holy Communion until we have confessed it).

Beyond this, the Church declares 'after having attained the age of discretion, each of the faithful is bound by an obligation faithfully to confess serious sins once a year' (*Catechism*, 1457). We should not waste too much time working out whether our sins are 'serious' or not. At some level, every sin is serious since it is an offence against a good and loving God, our Father. Surely every Catholic will want to perform at least this minimum requirement of an annual Confession. Lent is a very common (and appropriate) time to do this, but it can be done at any time.

However, as we have already said, Confession is not something we should put off or do as infrequently as possible. It is a privilege, a unique opportunity to receive the love and mercy of God. As such we should strive to make it a regular and frequent part of our spiritual lives.

Trying to go to Confession at least monthly is a good practise. We should confess not only mortal sins, but also venial sins if we can remember them, particularly those which form a habit in our lives - things like gossip, selfishness, resentment, impurity, anger, impatience, dishonesty. These bad habits ('vices') will take time to break down, but with God's help they can be vanquished, and Confession is a great help to this.

Making a good Confession

We have already spoken about the importance of making a regular Examination of Conscience. A simple Examination is included below - obviously everyone will have their own sins. The key to making a good Confession is generosity - always be totally honest with God. Never be afraid to confess a sin through embarrassment or pride. Remember that the priest is bound to secrecy by the Seal of Confession, and that he has probably heard far greater sins than yours.

Prayer before Confession

Lord Jesus, open my mind and my heart to your Holy Spirit. Help me to remember my sins. Help me to be sorry for them, and to make up my mind never to sins again. Holy Mary, Mother of God, pray for me that I may make a good Confession.

A simple examination of conscience

1. 'You shall love the Lord your God with all your heart'

- Have I been loyal to the teachings of the Church?
- Have I betrayed my faith or put it at risk?
- Am I faithful to my daily prayers?
- Have I put my trust in superstition or the Occult?
- Have I cursed, sworn, or broken my word?
- Did I deliberately miss Mass on any Sunday or Holyday of Obligation?
- Did I fulfil my Easter duties?
- Have I ever withheld something I ought to have confessed?

2. 'You shall love your neighbour as yourself?'

- Have I respected my parents and those in authority?
- Have I neglected my family responsibilities?
- Have I got drunk, been greedy, used drugs or pornography?
- Have I been lazy at work, in study or at home?
- Have I been impure, by myself or with others?
- Have I used forms of birth control forbidden by the Church?
- Have I cheated, stolen or gambled beyond my means?
- Have I told lies to excuse myself or injure others?

Procedure in Confession

Begin by saying:
'Bless me, Father, for I have sinned. It is a week/month (state length of time) since my last Confession'.

Then tell the priest all the sins you can remember, and the number of times committed. When you have finished confessing all your sins you can say; 'I am sorry for all these sins and the sins of my past life'.

Then wait while the priest gives you any necessary advice, and gives you a penance. After this you say an *Act of Contrition*, for example:

'O my God, because you are so good, I am very sorry that I have sinned against you, and by the help of your grace I will not sin again'.

The priest then gives you *Absolution*:
'God the Father of mercies, through the death and resurrection of his Son, has reconciled the world to himself and sent the Holy Spirit among us for the forgiveness of sins. Through the ministry of the Church may God give you pardon and peace, and I absolve you from your sins in the Name of the Father, ✠ and of the Son and of the Holy Spirit. Amen.

Prayer after Confession

If possible, perform your penance before leaving church. You might like to add:

I thank you, my God, for having pardoned me. How worthy you are of my love! May I never offend you again. Mary, my Mother, and all you angels and saints, praise and thank the Lord for his goodness to me, a sinner.

The Sunday Gospels During Lent

The Sundays of Lent can be put into three groups.

(a) The first two Sundays have two Gospel stories appropriate to Lent: Christ's fast in the wilderness and his Transfiguration. They are read from Matthew, Mark and Luke in yearly sequence, like the Gospel Readings on Sundays of Ordinary Time.

(b) The 3rd, 4th and 5th Sundays each have a Lenten theme. The readings of Year A come from John. They are about baptism, because Lent is essentially a time of preparation for the great baptism service at the Easter Vigil. Because they are so important, they may also be used in Years B and C. Readings for Year B look forward to Holy Week as the great celebration of Christ's Passion and death. Again they are taken from John. In Year C the readings are about penitence and forgiveness. They are taken from Luke and John.

(c) The last Sunday in Lent is Passion (or Palm) Sunday. It is also the beginning of Holy Week. (See p. 57)

1st Sunday - Jesus fasts for 40 days

Every year we begin the fast of Lent with the story of Our Lord's 40-day fast in the wilderness, preparing himself for his work as Messiah and giving us an example of victory over temptation. Our own 40 days of Lent prepare us for Easter and the solemn celebration of Baptism for new Christians, the great sacrament of our Redemption in which sin is rejected by us and forgiven by God. We learn to celebrate Lent by joining with Jesus in fasting, prayer and unselfishness.

Year A: Matthew 6:1-6. 16-18
This is the most familiar account of Christ's testing in the wilderness. The devil tempts him to do what he came into the world to do (feed his people, show God's wondrous power, and reign over the world) but for the wrong reasons. His quotations from the Old Testament carry undertones of the story of Israel's 40 years of hardship and preparation in the wilderness after they escaped from Egypt. The correspondence between the salvation of the Israelites from Egypt and Christ's salvation of the whole world re-appears in the Easter Vigil readings.

Year B: Mark 1:12-15
Mark's concise account does not spell out the Lord's temptations in detail, but mentions the angels and wild

animals that were with him - to which Matthew and Luke allude in their quotations from Psalm 90. Here the Second Adam (1 *Cor* 15:22) is with angels and animals, not in a garden, like the first Adam, but in a wasteland; and how different is his response to temptation!

Year C: Luke 4:1-13
Luke has a different order for the three temptations, bringing the Temple into prominence by giving it the last place. This is the Gospel that begins and ends in the Temple, with which Jesus identified himself. He saw himself as replacing the Temple as the sign of God's presence in the world.

2nd Sunday - The Transfiguration

After Peter, on behalf of all the apostles, has acknowledged that Jesus is the Messiah, Jesus prepares his disciples for his own suffering, death and resurrection. He lets them see his true glory in a vision that recalls his baptism by John in the river Jordan. This reading prepares us for both the Passion and for Easter.

Year A: Matthew 17:1-19
Matthew's account stresses the glory and power of the transfigured Lord. Only Matthew compares Christ's face to the dazzling splendour of the sun, and has Jesus saying 'Do not be afraid.'

Year B: Mark 9:2-10
Mark adds that after the Transfiguration the disciples were still puzzled about what he meant by 'rising from the dead'.

Year C: Luke 9:28b-36
Luke specifically states that Jesus talks with Moses and Elijah about his forthcoming 'passing (or exodus) at Jerusalem', meaning his Passion and death.

3rd Sunday

Looking forward to the Paschal Baptism

Year A: John 4:5-42 - The woman at the well
Christ promises living waters to the Samaritan woman at the well of Sychar. These waters are experienced in Baptism, the great sacrament of faith, for which we are preparing at Easter.

Looking forward to Holy Week

Year B: John 2:13-25 - The cleansing of the Temple
John places this event near the beginning of the Lord's ministry, but the other gospels place it shortly before he is arrested. What he says on this occasion will be repeated on the Cross. The Temple he cleanses is that of the human soul and of the Church.

Penitence and forgiveness

Year C: Luke 13:1-9 - Jesus warns of God's wrath
Pilate has recently had some Galileans killed in Jerusalem. Jesus recalls them as he approaches Jerusalem for the last time, knowing that Pilate will soon crucify him. He declares the Kingdom of God has arrived, that his Passion is imminent. Then in the parable of the fig tree, he reminds the disciples that God gives everyone time for penitence to prepare for death and judgement.

4th Sunday

Looking forward to the Paschal Baptism

Year A: John 9:1-49 - Curing the man born blind
Jesus gives sight to the blind man by washing his eyes. This parallels the instruction of catechumens preparing for baptism at Easter. Sight is a symbol of faith, and the man comes to believe in Jesus through this healing. The Jews begin planning to kill Jesus.

Looking forward to Holy Week

Year B: John 3:14-21 - The bronze serpent
During their 40 years in the wilderness, God healed the Israelites when a bronze serpent, symbol of wisdom, was hung up on a pole for them to see. The whole world will be healed when it sees Jesus, the power and wisdom of God, hung on a cross.

Penitence and forgiveness

Year C: Luke 15:1-3.11-32 - The prodigal son

This great story of God's forgiveness helps us to prepare for Easter by meditating on God's love. The Father loves both sons equally, in spite of their different sins.

5th Sunday

Looking forward to the Paschal Baptism

Year A: John 11:1-45 - The raising of Lazarus

Christ is now very near to Jerusalem. By recalling Lazarus from the tomb, though not a resurrection to eternal life, Jesus shows God's power over death. This will be fully shown by the resurrection of Jesus. Christ's resurrection is the heart of our faith.

Looking forward to Holy Week

Year B: John 12:20-33 - A grain of wheat must die

Like wheat that must die and be buried to produce grain, Jesus must die in order to rise in glory and take his disciples with him. The disciples must be ready to die too.

Penitence and forgiveness

Year C: John 8:1-11 - A woman taken in adultery

This incident is part of the prelude to Christ's passion. During his last days, some Pharisees try to trick Jesus about an adulterous woman. He concentrates on the

Pharisees and teaches them to forgive. He does not absolve her sins (she shows neither faith nor repentance), but he refuses to condemn her to punishment - which according strictly to the Law would mean death.

Holy Week - Liturgy and Word

The celebration of Holy Week begins with Passion (or Palm) Sunday, continues through the first half of the week with ordinary daily mass and hours of prayer, culminating in the Three Great Holy Days from Holy Thursday evening to Easter Sunday afternoon.

Passion Sunday - The story of the Passion

Today's liturgy has two parts:

(a) *The palms procession* The mass begins with a solemn procession with palms, recalling the entry of Jesus to Jerusalem riding on a donkey, a few days before he is arrested. Because of this the day is commonly called Palm Sunday; but we should not sentimentalise the donkey The donkey is a sign of poverty and lowliness, exactly right for the King who shares all the world's suffering and redeems its misery. Each year this story is read from the Gospel of the Year, Matthew, Mark, or Luke.

(b) *Mass of the passion.* During the mass the story of the Passion is read from the same gospel. Each Reading tells the same story, which has six sections:

(1) Three preliminary incidents: Judas promises to betray Jesus; a woman anoints his feet at Bethany; and the Last Supper.
(2) Jesus is arrested after he prays in the garden of Gethsemane.
(3) The Jewish Grand Council interrogates Jesus and decides to hand him over to the Roman Governor, who alone can give the death sentence.
(4) The Governor, Pontius Pilate, tries Jesus and condemns him to death.
(5) Jesus is crucified.
(6) His body is placed in the tomb.

Year A: Matthew 26:14-27:77

This is the longest Passion reading and the one with most quotations from the Old Testament. It includes Pilate washing his hands in a hypocritical gesture, and the story of his wife's dream. Matthew also tells of the crowd's hatred of Jesus, of others rising from the dead at time of the crucifixion, and of Pilate setting a guard on the tomb. Because of the length, the story of the anointing at Bethany is omitted here, but it is read in John's version on Monday.

Year B: Mark 14:1-15:1-47

This is the starkest account of the Passion and, because other people are so little mentioned, it emphasizes the impression of Jesus being utterly deserted and alone. Only Mark tells of the young man who was stripped during the scuffle when Jesus is arrested in Gethsemane, and only Mark ends the story with the three Marys at the tomb.

Year C: Luke 22:14-23:56
In Luke's account, Christ's concern for others makes him appear serene, and we have fuller and more frequent mention of his prayers. Luke tells of the angel in Gethsemane and of Christ being taken to see Herod. The Lord's words to the women of the city, his prayer for his executioners and his promise to the penitent thief are all in this account only. Luke puts the anointing at Bethany in a different chapter, which will be read at mass tomorrow. After the Lord's entrance to Jerusalem on Sunday, an uneasy calm reigns. Mass is said daily, but without special ceremonies.

Monday

John 12:1-11: Six days before the Sabbath on which his body will lie in the tomb, a woman anoints Jesus in the house at Bethany. Reckoning in Jewish style, today is six days before Holy Saturday.

Tuesday

John 13:21-33. 36-38: This passage is taken out of time sequence in order to show that Jesus fully accepts that

Judas will betray him and Peter will disown him, but prays to the Father for his coming glorification on the cross.

Wednesday

Matthew 26:14-25: This day is often called 'Spy Wednesday' because today Judas accepts the thirty pieces of silver from the priests. The Gospel Reading consists of the opening sentences of St Matthew's Passion account. Jesus declares that his 'hour', which he has looked forward to since the wedding at Cana, has now arrived.

The three great holy days

These three days, often referred to in Latin as *Triduum Sacrum*, are reckoned in Jewish fashion, each day beginning at sundown (Genesis describes a day as 'evening and morning'.) They run from the Thursday evening liturgy to sundown on Easter Sunday.

Holy Thursday

Mass is celebrated only once in any church, in the evening, to recall the Last Supper. After the homily, the bishop or priest washes the feet of several people before the altar, vividly recalling Jesus washing the disciples' feet. This action is the perfect expression of God's purpose in the Incarnation and Redemption, because washing the feet of others expresses readiness to suffer and to die, both in Jesus and in us.

After the mass the Blessed Sacrament for the next day's communion is taken to a place where people can pray before it until later that night, in response to our Lord begging the disciples to watch with him in Gethsemane.

Good Friday

This morning and tomorrow every one is encouraged to attend the Office of Readings and Morning Prayer in church.

The solemn liturgy of the day takes place in the afternoon, at the time of Christ's death. It has no splendour and no happy hymns.

The first part begins with reading of the Passion according to John, the shortest of the four accounts of the Lord's trial and death. It is also the most dramatic and affecting. It contains more of the dialogue between the Lord and Pilate about Christ's kingship; Our Lady at the cross; Christ's thirst; and the blood and water flowing from his side after death. It is followed by solemn prayers for the whole world.

The second part is the unveiling of a big wooden cross. Everybody is invited to kneel before it and kiss it, as an act of love and faith.

The third part is the saying of the Lord's Prayer. Holy Communion for all, in the form of the Sacred Body only, follows as an act of union with the crucified Lord.

Holy Saturday - Easter Vigil

No mass is celebrated on this day. The quietness dramatically reminds us of Christ's body resting in the tomb.

But when darkness comes, we hold the most important and beautiful liturgy of the whole year. We meet outside the church for the blessing of new fire, from which a big candle, decorated with five grains of incense to commemorate Christ's wounds, is lit. As we are led into the church by this great candle, the darkness is dispersed by lighting everybody's hand-candles from it. Thus the light of Christ fills the whole world, carried by Christians.

Four or more readings from Holy Scripture then tell the story of God's love for us from the creation onwards till all is fulfilled in the Resurrection of Christ. One of the readings is always the story of the Israelites being saved by the waters of the Red Sea, which typifies our salvation through faith and baptism. Baptismal water is blessed for the year; and if there are new Christians to be baptised or received into communion, they are baptised and received.

Then the bells and the organ peal out, as we begin the first mass of Easter, thanking God for Christ's victory over death and sin during this holy night.

Another Lent has ended, with exuberant joy of music and flowers, in the presence of the Risen Christ. This is *the* day of all the year.

"40-3-50"

After 40 days of preparation during Lent, there are these 3 days if intense celebration of the Lord's Passover, followed by 50 days of joy and feasting to Pentecost and the coming of the Holy Spirit.

STEPS TO DAILY PRAYER IN LENT

Pope John Paul II is reported to have said: 'Any method of prayer is valid insofar as it is inspired by Christ and leads to Christ who is the Way, the Truth, and the Life' (*Jn* 14:6).

"To be sure, there are as many paths of prayer as there are persons who pray, but it is the same Spirit acting in all and with all." (*Catechism*, 2672)

A heartfelt response

True as these words are, for us to consider a 'method of prayer' - perhaps a different approach to prayer during Lent from those we are already familiar with - can be misleading. To adopt a method of prayer can indicate that we are searching for a good way to tackle an activity which may be rather difficult, *and that when we have mastered this approach, we will have achieved our goal*. However, it is not the mastering of 'prayer techniques' which is our goal. Prayer is not like learning to fly, so that when we have put in all the hours and passed the tests we can say, "Look! I'm doing it! I've succeeded." Prayer is simply the response we make to the continual, incessant call of God to our hearts. "God's breath in man returning to his birth" as George Herbert put it. It will help, of course, to ensure our response is frequent and appropriate so that it becomes natural and habitual, especially in difficult times, but the method is not the goal. It is God who is the light to which we turn, the warmth in which we bask and the water of life which we drink. God is our natural element which our whole selves breathe in, like the air our bodies need. In him, as St. Paul tells us, we live and move and have our being (*Acts* 17:28). Jesus Christ is our means to this; he is himself the way we travel to God, the truth by which we distinguish truth from error as we go, and the life itself which he shares with the Father, and offers to us. We are enabled to do this by "the Holy Spirit, whose anointing permeates our whole being, ... the interior Master of Christian prayer." (*Catechism*, 2672) It is God himself who is our way and our goal.

A turning to God

Lent, however, is a good time to take stock of our response to God's call to us. A time when we can consider to what extent the approach to prayer we have at this part of our lives is actually enabling us to respond to him and to our fellow men. Whatever variation of form or aim there may be in our prayer, if it does not lead to a constant, if almost imperceptible, Godward realignment of our selves and our lives, it has not been effective. In turning towards God, it is not he who is moved or changed by our blessings and adoration, our petitions and intercessions or even our thanksgiving; it is we who, in turning and re-turning to him, are reconfigured through his power to his love.

"Prayer and Christian life are inseparable, for they concern the same love and the same renunciation, proceeding from love; the same filial and loving conformity with the Father's plan of love; the same transforming union in the Holy Spirit who conforms us more and more to Christ Jesus; the same love for all men, the love with which Jesus has loved us." (*Catechism*, 2745)

Steps to Prayer

During the days of Lent, as we prepare for the events of Holy Week and Easter, it is possible to focus on many different ways of prayer at different times. Two of the several forms of prayer are represented here, those of *petition* and *intercession* which are perhaps those which come most naturally to us. We are assured by Jesus himself that whatever we ask the Father in his name will be given to us (*Jn* 15:16-17) and so the following thoughts and prayers are concentrated on aspects of our life with God which we know he wishes us to possess ever more fully.

Our dependency

God is the creator and we are creatures. We have not caused ourselves to live, we do not control most of the circumstances of our lives and we cannot choose its final ending. God is entirely 'other'; outside of his creation and holding every part of it in being constantly, yet an intimate part of it as well, through the Incarnation of his Son Jesus. In turning to God, whether that movement is a sudden leap or one of many gentle realignments, we acknowledge our own dependency, our own mortality, but we are not alone even as we do this. God himself has shared this humanity, this weakness and dependency. He himself is both companion and destination.

Lord, you alone are the source of my life and its final end. Keep me within the circle of your eternal love so that, whichever way I turn, it may be towards you.

Our infidelity

Inevitably, the first acknowledgement that we must make in turning towards God is that we have previously been turned away from him to some degree. Our turning Godwards is in itself a recognition that we have fallen short in being receptive to the life that flows from the Creator, and an acknowledgement that we cannot remain completely oriented to him without constantly needing his help.

Lord, forgive me for the times I have allowed myself to turn away from you. Keep me in the light of your presence, for in you there is no shadow of turning at all.

Our coming back

Once we have aligned ourselves with God and acknowledged that we have previously turned ourselves away, however slightly, from his Fatherly love, we need to reorient our prayer with his intentions. As baptised Christians, we are called to help bring about the Kingdom of God both here and now and in the future, thus we join our prayer with that of the whole Church, even when we pray alone.

> Lord, guide the days and the years of my life. Help me to grow in receptiveness to the gentle promptings of your Spirit so that all I think and all I do may be used for the coming of your Kingdom.

Bringing our needs

In turning Godwards, we not only bring our failings to him, but also our needs and difficulties which we lay open to his light and loving care. Open to his light, we can bring anything at all before him. It makes no difference whether the problem is finding a parking space or managing terrible debts; once we have turned honestly to God through Jesus who is the truth itself, we can be confident of beginning on a truth-centred solution.

> Lord, you know my every need. In Christ your Son you assumed all the intricate difficulties of human

life. I bring to you every need of my life, however small, so that you may direct my choices towards the light of your love.

The needs of others

In praying for our own needs, we find it natural to incorporate the needs of others in prayers of intercession. It is Jesus himself who is the one intercessor with the Father on behalf of us all, so in praying for others, we must necessarily join with him and with the Holy Spirit who intercedes for us. "The prayer of Jesus makes Christian prayer an efficacious petition. He is its model, he prays in us and with us. Since the heart of the Son seeks only what pleases the Father, how could the prayer of the children of adoption be centered on the gifts rather than the Giver?" (*Catechism*, 2740)

Lord, I bring to you those I hold in my heart; some are dear to me and all are in need. As the days lengthen towards Easter, let your Holy Spirit encourage and strengthen them and turn them towards your light and love.

In need of mercy

John Donne speaks of the mercy of God as "that which is older than our beginning, and shall over-live our end". In our prayer for others, we accept our connection to the whole Church in the communion of saints and we recognize our dependence on God's mercy towards us and to those we love.

> Lord, there are no limits to your love and mercy, though when I turn from your light, I may cease to recognize your goodness in the shadows of my life. Call those I love and those who are in need into the warmth of your mercy so they may understand that you are yourself the answer.

For the salvation of all

All creation is enclosed within the love of God, so in turning to him, we are able to intercede through Jesus, enabled by the gentle urgings of the Holy Spirit, for all men, even those who would do us harm. There are no boundaries to God's mercy, so there can be none in our prayer.

> Lord, your mercy knows no beginning or end. Call those who live in the shadow of hatred or unbelief into the healing light of your presence. I join my prayers for the salvation of all who reject you to those of your holy Mother and all the communion of saints.

Understanding the Stations of the Cross

The history of the Stations

After the Franciscans were given care of the Holy Places in Jerusalem in 1342, the custom grew of stopping to pray at various places on the route which Jesus walked during his sacred Passion. This devotion was enriched with indulgences.

Travelling to Jerusalem was much more difficult in those days and before long, there was a desire to reproduce scenes from our Lord's Way of the Cross in Churches in Europe. The Stations became popular in the late 17th century after the Popes began to grant indulgences for those who made this devotion. The number and subject of the Stations varied until the scheme of our present fourteen Stations was stabilised by Pope Clement XII in 1731.

During the following twenty years, St Leonard of Port Maurice enthusiastically promoted the Stations and it is said that he saw to the erection of 572 sets of Stations in various Churches during that period. Now most Churches in Europe have a set of Stations of the Cross, varying from a set of simple wooden crosses (the essential requirement), to recognised works of art in various styles.

How to pray the Stations

There are no set prayers for the Stations of the Cross. All that is required is to move from one Station to the next and to pause for a time at each one, to meditate on the passion and death of Our Lord. If a group of people makes the Stations, led by a priest or another person, it is sufficient for the leader to move from one Station to the next (in some Churches it is not practical for everyone to move to each Station.)

Although there are no set prayers required, many people find it helpful to use a prayer book with a set of readings for each Station. The most famous series of meditations is that composed by St Alphonsus Liguori. He gives a "consideration" for each station in which we think about how, for example, it was not Pilate but our sins that truly condemned Jesus to die. He gives a prayer related to each consideration, in which we ask for various graces to avoid sin and lead a good life.

There are very many different booklets and schemes which people have written to accompany the Stations of the Cross. Many use texts from the Holy Scriptures to help us, others are written for people in particular states of life or for those in various circumstances. On Good Friday each year, the Holy Father makes the Stations of the Cross at the Colosseum in Rome. The Vatican publishes the scripture texts that are used, together with the meditations and prayers so that the faithful can use them for their own devotion.

At the end of each Station, it is usual to say an act of contrition and perhaps the Our Father, Hail Mary and Glory be. However, it is in the nature of the Stations that they can be adapted to suit different needs. For example, a priest who leads a group of schoolchildren in making this devotion might make each Station fairly briefly.

Fruits of this devotion

As with all our prayers and devotions, the purpose of making the Stations of the Cross is to adore, God, thank Him, express our sorrow to Him and to ask him for the grace to change our lives for the better. Meditating on the passion of Our Lord is encouraged by the Church because it helps us so much.

God loves us infinitely. Original sin and the personal sins of each individual made a gulf between us and his love. Nevertheless, he sent his only Son to redeem us and to win back for us the grace we need to enjoy his presence for ever in heaven. He has given us wonderful gifts of grace in Baptism, Confirmation and the Holy Eucharist.

Nevertheless, we continue to sin against him. During his Passion, Our Lord was aware of the sins of the whole world and suffered in agony because of these sins, including our own personal sins. When we make the Stations of the Cross, we reflect on these truths so that we can renew our love and gratitude for Our Lord's sacrifice, and so that we can be more heartily and genuinely sorry for our sins. By thinking of the falls of Jesus, his scourging, his being nailed to the Cross, we can make a more determined effort to avoid sin in the future and to offer our prayers, penances and good deeds in union with his own offering of his life for us on the Cross.

As well as our own sins, we also offer our sorrow to Jesus for the sins of the world. We know of poverty and injustice in the world, caused by human sin. In our own country, the "culture of death" allows unborn children to be killed and threatens the elderly and the vulnerable. Our Lord is in anguish at these evils: at the Stations, we can try to console him, perhaps offering to make some sacrifice in union with his.

Many of the great saints wrote about the Passion of Christ because they understood how fruitful this devotion is, and how much it can enrich our spiritual life. The Stations of the Cross help us to follow their good example.

Indulgences attached

The Church continues to encourage us to make the Stations of the Cross. She grants us the possibility of obtaining a Plenary Indulgence each day for making this devotion. If we are ill or for some other reason cannot physically make the Stations of the Cross, we can gain the indulgence by using some readings or meditations on the Passion of Our Lord for some time, perhaps a quarter of an hour. An obvious way to do this would be to use a prayer book with some meditations on the Stations.

As with all Plenary Indulgences, to gain it, we must go to Holy Communion on the same day, go to Confession within a week or two before or after, and pray for the intentions of the Holy Father. The further condition is that we should be free of any attachment even to venial sin. This might seem impossible. However, the Sacred Penitentiary recently spoke of this as "having conceived a detestation of any sin whatsoever". This is not impossible for us. The Stations of the Cross, in fact, are the ideal devotion for us to conceive in our hearts a genuine detestation for any sin as we reflect devoutly on the Passion of Our Lord, the suffering that our sins have caused him, and the overflowing love and mercy with which he forgives us and invites us to live in his love.

Informative Catholic Reading

We hope that you have enjoyed reading this booklet.

If you would like to find out more about CTS booklets - we'll send you our free information pack and catalogue.

Please send us your details:

Name ....

Address ....

....

....

Postcode ....

Telephone...

Email ....

Send to: CTS, 40-46 Harleyford Road,
Vauxhall, London
SE11 5AY

Tel: 020 7640 0042
Fax: 020 7640 0046
Email: info@cts-online.org.uk